Persia / Iran

A Pictorial Treasury of Twenty-Five Centuries

A. E. Woolley

CHILTON BOOKS
A Division of Chilton Company, Publishers
PHILADELPHIA

AMPHOTO
American Photographic Book Publishing Co., Inc.
NEW YORK

To My Wife, Dorothy Ellen

Published in New York by Amphoto, and simultaneously, in Toronto, Canada, by Ambassador Books, Ltd. All rights reserved. No part of this book may be reproduced in any manner without the written consent of the publisher.

Library of Congress Catalog Card No. 65-23146

Printed in the United States of America

Acknowledgements

When one looks back on a completed project, there is usually a question that looms large, "How did I manage to get all of this done?" And when the question demands an answer, in order to properly thank those whose aid and contribution made the project successful, it is surprising how the list of contributors grows.

I am sure that my photographic study of PERSIA/IRAN could not have been completed without the invaluable assistance of the following people. These are not necessarily in the order of importance, for I would be at a loss to indicate the degree of my dependence on these individuals. From the beginning, Virgil and Irma DeWitt, Bill and Grace Pugliese, and Henry DuBois had confidence. Magazine assignments that supported the whole were done for Alexander Taylor of *MD* Magazine, Don Erickson of *Esquire,* and John Balcomb of UNICEF. And on the home front were Carl and Brita Reed, Ben and Vivian Karp, and Ken and Jean Green.

On the Iranian front, Americans and Iranians together made my tour of the country a pleasure and success. Mr. Henry L. Davis of the USIS office and his photographic lab employees, Alex Minasian, Mohamd Radfar, Monocher Parvin, Herayer Nazarian; Bob and Mimi McLaughlin of the USIS Khorramshahr office, and Ollie Jones.

The Ministry of Information served an inestimable intermediate role throughout the project. Under the direction of Mr. Ali-Asghar Armin Moez the office was able to fulfill every request, no matter how impossible, I made of them. Mr. P. Arbabi, who worked very closely with us, put himself fully into the work, and his organization of my demands requires a special note of appreciation. His Excellency, Mr. Husain Ghods-Nakhai, Minister of the Imperial Court, and his principal aide, Mr. Homayoun Bahadori, made it possible for the private audience with Shah Pahlavi and the royal family.

For a rescue from a frustrating situation in Abadan we owe a debt to Mr. C. Linne Carlson. Dr. Otto Lehner arranged for the journey into Nomad land with UNICEF and Malaria Control organizations. Dr. A. B. Ramazani of the Iranian Oil Company overcame holiday crowds to give us considerate attention.

The tour of duty in Isfahan was made interesting and successful because of the intelligent efforts of Mr. Kazem Hekmat Shear. Pleasant memories will linger for many years from this acquaintance. And in Shiraz we received help from Mr. Hasan Ali Moderres. In Tehran one man offered personal as well as professional aid. He was Victor Hagopian. Although the visit was short in the fishing center of Pahlavi, a special thanks must be given Karim Kazemi for showing us the operations of the fishing factory.

There are two men to whom appreciation must be offered for their contribution of assistance while we were working with the Nomads. The first man will have to remain nameless for he spoke no English. But his ability as a driver over the worst roads in Iran, where one is confronted with big overloaded trucks and racing buses at every blind curve (and there are curves every twenty yards, it seems), deserves highest praise. And for beds, breakfast, and a busy tour with the tribes, Mr. Fazlolh Rouhamy of the Kazaroon Medical Research Station deserves special mention.

There are others who made the journey a memorable one by their daily activities. These people are the ones who make up a city, town, village, or tribe. They made the book possible.

A. E. Woolley
New Paltz, New York

Table of Contents

The Art of Iran

by Dr. Hugo Munsterberg,
Professor of Art History,
State University of New York,
New Paltz, New York

On the tomb of King Darius, at Naqsh-i-Rustam in southern Iran, is an inscription that was cut into the rock almost 2,500 years ago. It says, "A great god is Ahuramazda, who created this earth, who created yonder sky, who created man, who created happiness for man, who made Darius king, one king of many, one lord of many.

"I am Darius the Great King, King of Kings, King of countries containing all kinds of men, King in this great earth far and wide, son of Hystaspes, an Achaemenian, a Persian, son of a Persian, an Aryan, having Aryan lineage." After listing the many countries he had conquered and ruled, the blessings of his reign, the towns he rebuilt, and the walls he constructed, the inscription concludes: "May Ahuramazda together with the gods protect me, and my royal house, and what has been inscribed by me."

This great king is dead. The Achaemenid house has given way to other ruling families. The empire they established, like all empires of this world, has vanished, but the magnificent tomb with its powerful sculptures can still be admired by all who make the trip to Fars.

And not too far from Naqsh-i-Rustam is the sacred city of Persepolis, which, even in ruins, is one of the great artistic sites in the world, comparable to the Acropolis or to the Roman Forum. Built during the late sixth and fifth centuries B.C., it is a lasting tribute to the glory of Achaemenid Persia. Under Darius the Great, and his successor, Xerxes, magnificent columned palaces and vast audience halls were built, which for grandeur of conception and beauty of execution had no equals in the contemporary world. Sculpture decorating their walls compare with the best of classical Greek carvings, and the decorative arts of the period, especially gold and silver vessels, are among the finest works of their kind.

Ancient Persia's golden age of art was merely the culmination of a long artistic development that had begun many centuries before. Modern archaeologists have traced the beginnings of Iranian art back to the neolithic pottery culture of the fourth millennium, when beautiful earthenware jars decorated with abstract and symbolical animal designs were made all over Iran. The more ancient cities are excavated, the more impressive becomes the picture of artistic production in these early stages of Persia's culture. Be it the Luristan bronzes with their animated linear designs (discovered a generation ago in graves of Western Iran) or marvelous clay animal figures found only recently on the shores of the Caspian Sea, all over the country new finds are constantly adding to the masterpieces of ancient Persian art, and untold treasures are undoubtedly still hidden in the soil.

Among all these discoveries, perhaps the single most dramatic was the gold treasure found at Ziwiye in northern Kurdistan in 1947. Dating from the early centuries of the first millennium, these artifacts are among the most splendid of their type—true masterpieces of the goldsmith's craft. Among them are solid gold beakers and cups, plaques and pectorals, necklaces and bracelets, and even animal sculptures in the round. All of them show a wonderful sense of design and the high level of craftsmanship that has been characteristic of Persian art throughout the ages. For it is in the decorative arts that Iran has always been most successful. And, it is no exaggeration to say that Persian craftsmen have elevated decorative art forms, all too often dismissed as minor works of little importance, to the level of a truly major art.

Although the ancient art of Persia came to an end when the Greeks conquered the Achaemenid empire and brought with them a provincial version of Hellenistic art, which for a time predominated, the great artistic tradition of the past, which had never wholly died out, experienced a revival under the native Sasanian dynasty, which ruled from the fourth to seventh centuries A.D. Magnificent palaces built of brick and decorated with stucco, now unfortunately almost completely destroyed, were erected by Sasanian kings—structures which were to have lasting influence on all Islamic architecture of the Near East. There were sculptural reliefs in imitation of those of Achaemenidian times, and wall paintings and mosaics were used to decorate palaces. Unfortunately, very little of this work has survived, but beautiful silver vessels and plates, and above all, silks indicate the sophisticated and refined culture that must have flourished in this age.

Conquest of the Sasanian empire by Arabs during the middle of the seventh century temporarily halted this great artistic florescence, but soon Islamic rulers, Arabs, Seljuk Turks, Mongols, and Turkish Timurids became enthusiastic patrons of Persian craftsmen. Architecture experienced a great revival, with elaborate tombs for dead rulers and magnificent mosques and madrases. Although painting and sculpture disappeared, since the Prophet had forbidden the making of human images, decorative arts again flourished. In fact, ceramics, glass, textiles, and metal work are considered among the best ever made in Persia, outstanding both for beauty of design and excellence of workmanship.

The last truly creative, and in some ways the most remarkable, period of Persian art was that of the Safavid dynasty, which ruled Iran from 1501 to 1734 A.D. It was during this time that famous Persian carpets were produced at places like Tabriz, Herat, Isfahan, Kashan, and the Caucasus, carpets which have rightly been considered the very epitome of this art form. In fact, the sixteenth and seventeenth century rugs became so popular that today the term "Persian Carpet" is used to describe certain types of rugs, whether or not they were actually made in Persia. The most celebrated of these masterpieces of Persian looms, originally made for palaces and mosques of Safavid Persia, are now on display in art museums throughout the world and are valued as highly as the great works of European paintings and sculpture.

Carpets, however, were only one aspect of Persian art of the time. Architecture, with its use of colored-tile-decorated domed structures, such as mosques and palaces in Isfahan, was also remarkable, and has certainly never been surpassed in beauty of color. Ceramics continued to flourish, although they lacked some of the strength and animation of earlier Islamic pottery. And a new art form which had developed under the Mongols, miniature painting, came into full flower and had its golden age under the Timurid and Safavid rulers. These paintings, small in scale but exquisite in execution, with their flat, ornamental designs and brilliant colors, are among the masterpieces of illuminated miniatures. Dealing with legends and history of Iran, which they portray in a very sophisticated style, Persian miniatures are a fitting climax to the ancient artistic tradition of Iran, which is one of the oldest and most remarkable in the world.

An Outline History of Iran

by Dr. S. R. Shafagh
University of Tehran

Iran, or Persia, is a part of a great plateau that comprises a total area of about 2,600,000 square kilometers. Of this area, the present Iran has only 1,600,000. The population is 22,000,000, of which some seventy percent is rural. The common language is Persian, which belongs to the Iranian branch of Indo-European languages. The religion is Islam.

Not long after immigration of the Arians, which took place during the beginning of the second millennium b.c., the Iranian communities settled and formed local kingdoms like those of Mada (*Gr.* Media) on the North West, Soghda, and Bactria on the North East.

HAKHAMANESHI EMPIRE

The first national empire was founded by Kurush (*Gr.* Cyrus) about 559 b.c., who united different parts of the country and annexed Lydia and Babylon to his dominions, which extended from the Mediterranean to Sind. Few kings have left behind so noble a reputation as that which attaches to the memory of Kurush. A great leader of men, he was generous, benevolent, and did not think of forcing subject nations into a single mold, but had the wisdom to leave unchanged the institutions of each land he annexed to his crown. Persians called him "father"; Hellenes, whom he conquered, regarded him as "master" and "law-giver"; and Jews considered him "the annointed of the Lord." Kurush was the real founder of the Hakhamaneshi Dynasty (*Gr.* Achaemenian).

Kurush was succeeded by his eldest son, Cambujieh (*Gr.* Cambyses), who ruled from 530-522 b.c. He conquered Egypt and had Pharaoh Sammethicus III deported to Shush (*Gr.* Susa).

The greatest of Hakhamaneshis was undoubtedly Dariush (*Gr.* Darius), who reigned from 522-486 b.c. During his first years he devoted his time and energy to putting down disturbances that had shaken the country. And he re-established the unity of the Empire, which stretched from Egypt to Jaxartes.

Darius introduced the first international administration in history by forming a just government and maintaining law and order. He created an efficient taxation system. And he built a network of roads connecting East and West for the first time, the roads being the prototype of the via Roma. The main Royal Road stretched from Susa over Artbela and Harran to Ephesus. One thousand six hundred and seventy-seven miles long, the Royal Road was divided into one hundred and eleven post stations. Royal envoys covered it in a week. Darius did not neglect the sea way. He ordered that a canal be constructed connecting the Nile with the Red Sea, a forerunner to the Suez Canal. Scylax of Caryanda was given the task of sailing down the Indus and exploring a way to Egypt. The first main military achievement of Darius was the Scythian campaign, which took him as far as the Danube. Then came his famous drive against the mainland of Greece.

In his policy he followed the humanitarian rule of Kurush. He held in high esteem every vassal nation. He did not fail to provide his Empire with a legal framework and never forgot to preoccupy himself with the welfare of nations whose destinies he directed. Ahuramazda, the great God, was his guide. His constructive work, including buildings, palaces (like those in Susa and Persepolis), roads, and bridges, was as masterly as it was extensive.

Among Darius' successors, his son, Khshayarsha (*Gr.* Xerxes), 485-464 B.C., preferred to direct his energy to building palaces and monuments, but yielding to pressure from his generals, he decided to invade Greece. At the head of an army composed of forty-six nations and commanded by twenty-nine generals, Xerxes set out for Greece and took possession of Athens. He was, however, compelled to withdraw.

Ardashir (*Gr.* Artaxerxes), 464-424 B.C. continued the policy of Kurush and Darius by offering protection to all those oppressed and tolerating subject peoples' beliefs and laws. He permitted Ezra to restore to Jerusalem the Jewish families that were in exile, work that had already begun under Kurush, thus enabling Jews to re-establish themselves and compile their traditions. He actually sent Nehemiah, his cupbearer, to settle their differences, thus helping the Jews to regain their national life, as we read in the books of Nehemiah and Ezra of the Old Testament.

The reign of Hakhamaneshi kings came to an end with the tragic defeat of Darius III, 336-330 B.C., by Alexander of Macedonia. He was the eleventh and last of Hakhamaneshi rulers.

Alexander regarded himself as legitimate head of the Persian Empire and therefore adopted the dress and ceremonials of the Persian Kings. He began his world conquest with the ambition of founding a universal empire and drove as far as India. But in the summer of 326 B.C. his army compelled him to return home. He and his generals adopted Persian manners and customs and married Persian women. After his unexpected death in Babylon in 323 B.C., one of his generals, Seleucus Nicator, assumed leadership and founded the Seleucus dynasty (*Gr.* Seleucid), which ruled approximately a century. The rulers were Persianized by marriage and training. This kingdom was superseded by the Parthian dynasty, which sprang from an eastern nomadic tribe and managed to reign until about 224 A.D., *i.e.*, for a period of 400 years. The dynasty is named after its founder, Arshaka (*Gr.* Arsaces). This new national empire was consolidated by conquests of kings like Mehrdad I (*Gr.* Mithradates), Mehrdad II, and Farhad III (*Gr.* Pharaates). To all appearances Parthian rule was a continuation of Hakhamaneshi dominion, but in reality it never attained the glory nor the vast, well unified, and well organized empire of the great dynasty. There were some minor states that ruled independently and simultaneously with Parthian kings in different sections of the country. And there were continuous civil wars. There was also a good deal of Hellenism in Iran during that period, as the aftermath of the reign of Alexander and his successors. At the same time, the rise of the Parthian Empire marks the beginning of reaction against Hellenism and revival of Iranian traditions.

SASANIAN EMPIRE

The last great king of the Parthians was Ardawan V (*Gr.* Arthabanes), who inflicted massive defeat on the Roman Emperor Caracalla (217 A.D.) and his general Macrinus, compelling Rome to make big territorial concessions and pay heavy indemnity. But, concurrently, a new dynasty arose in Persia proper under a great personality called Ardashir (*Gr.* Artaxerxes), who founded the Sasanian Empire (*Gr.* Sasanids 226-651 A.D.).

Among some thirty rulers of this great and last pre-Islamic dynasty there were many accomplishments with enduring effect. Ardashir, who was crowned in 226, considered himself the legitimate Hakhamaneshi successor, and after smashing his enemies at home, he attempted consolidation of his frontiers. Conflict with Rome seemed inevitable, and so the first of the second series of Roman wars began in his reign, ending in reoccupation by the Persians of the two fortresses of Nisibis and Carrhea. During a reign of nearly 50 years Ardashir succeeded in building up a new world. His greatest achievement was to forge a mighty, well-organized army, which made possible his vast scheme of re-establishing another powerful and unified Empire. He also made Zarathustrianism the state religion. Shapur I (241-271), the son of Ardashir and the second of the three foremost kings of the dynasty, continued the war against Rome and captured Emperor Valerian. Khosrow I (531-579) is recognized as the greatest ruler of the line. He restored full power of the monarchy and introduced many administrative and social reforms. An extensive legislation was effected, irrigation projects were carried out, learning was encouraged, and translations were made from Greek and Sanskrit into Persian. Tolerance was practiced toward different faiths. Yazadgird III (632-651), the last Sasanian monarch, struggled in vain against the rising tide of Islam, and spent the last ten years of his life a hunted fugitive, much like Darius III of the Hakhamaneshi Empire.

ISLAMIC PERIOD

Khosraw Parvis (590-628), twenty-second ruler of the Sasanian dynasty, waged a series of wars against Rome in the course of which his armies advanced as far as Kadiqoy (*Gr.* Calcedon) opposite Constantinople, and occupied Syria, Damascus, Jerusalem, and Egypt. Roman armies reformed under Heraclius and took revenge, penetrating as far as Mesopotamia. Meanwhile, as the result of long, fruitless struggles, both parties were utterly enfeebled. It was during this period of exhaustion that a new power rose in Arabia. And in the year of the coronation of Yazdgird III (633), the first Arab squadron made its entry into Iranian territory. In the last decisive battle of a series of wars of Nehavend (641), Iran was defeated, and her political integrity was suspended for about 200 years. Iranians were converted to Islam in a comparatively short time. Only about 100,000 remained loyal to the old faith.

During Arab rule there were constant troubles and various uprisings within different sections of the Persian nation. The first effective blow was dealt by Umavi (*Gr.* Omavyad) Caliphate and helped to set up the House of Abbas (*Gr.* Abbasids). In 820 A.D. an Iranian general, Tahiris, who helped the Caliph Maamoun to fight against his brother Amin and was given governorship of Khorsan, succeeded in establishing a practically independent national dynasty. Tahiris fell before Yaakub, the founder of the Saffari dynasty, which in turn was superseded by the Samani House (900-1229), which formed the first strong Persian kingdom since the Sasanians.

The Samanians reigned over most of Persia and Transoxiana. Under their rule scholarship and arts flourished, and Persian poetry began to develop. This dynasty fell before the Ghaznavis (962-1186). The one strong ruler of the Ghaznavis was Mahmud, who invaded India several times between 1001 and 1024 and captured Transoxiana. His encouragement of art and science was no less remarkable. He founded a Madrassa in Ghazna and drew together men of letters, the poet Ferdowsi one of them. Mahmud's son, Masaud, fell to the Seljuks, who formed another and more lasting dynasty (1037-1300). The Seljuk Empire was the greatest since Arab conquest, extending between Byzantium and India. Persian science and literature flourished during the period. Malekshah (1072-1092) established an astronomical observatory in which Omar Khayyam and other men of science were employed to make calculations for a new calendar. He adorned his capital, Isfahan, with its many fine buildings. Seljuk power was attacked and smashed by the Mugul *(Gr.* Mongol) invasion that began about 1219 and lasted until 1335. Islam and Iran modified much of the character of the invaders, even making some of them patrons of art and learning. Historians like Rashiduddin, philosophers like Tusi, and poets like Attar, Roumi, and Saadi flourished contemporarily with these rulers. Iran got another strong and unifying force in the Safavi dynasty.

SAFAVI PERIOD

The Safavi period (1499-1736) was marked by deep-seated national revival in all aspects. Shah Abbas the Great (1582-1628) took a fitting place among famous rulers of that time which included Sulayman the Magnificent of Turkey, Akbar Shah of India, Charles V of the Holy Roman Empire, and Elizabeth I of England. He won distinction in his campaigns, made Isfahan his capital, and built magnificent mosques, palaces, roads, and canals. Caravanserais were constructed by his order all over the country.

The Safavis were followed by the Afshars, Zandies and Qajars. Nadir Shah, founder of the Afshar dynasty (1736-1747), invaded India and marched into Dehli *(Gr.* Delhi), and through his military genius formed a strong Empire, although not a lasting one.

The Qajar period (1779-1925) is noted for disastrous defeats before the Russian invasions during the reign of Fathali Shah that led to the ignominious treaties of Gulistan (1813) and Turkaman Chai (1828) involving the total loss of Caucasus and "capitulations" granted to Russia.

PAHLAVI PERIOD

The last years of Qajar rule, due to ineptitude of those in authority and devastations caused by the first world war, were most critical years. It was in such critical times that Reza Shah rose to power and ascended to the throne of Persia in 1925, founding the Pahlavi dynasty. Reza Shah, who felt more keenly than perhaps any other Iranian the tragic contrast between Iran's glorious past and her existing backwardness, resolved to rouse the country from her lethargy. He created a new army with modern weapons, smothered all foreign provocations, and established order in all corners of the country. He advocated and instituted better education.

Iran threw off all foreign infiltration, abolished so-called "capitulations," and recovered her legitimate rights. In short, Reza Shah's one cordial desire was a national revival and true modernization of his country.

Today, His Imperial Majesty Mohammad Reza Shah Pahlavi is the leading spirit and a monarch determined to realize the systematic development of his country in many different ways. He has begun a new democracy by putting six cardinal propositions before his people:

1. Abolition of the landlord-serf system of agriculture.
2. Nationalization of forests.
3. Sales of shares in government-owned factories to underwrite land reforms.
4. Profit-sharing for workers in industrial and productive units.
5. Creation of a "Literacy Corps" to provide teachers in the first phases of compulsory national education.
6. New election laws with the declared aim of eliminating corruption and guaranteeing democratic representation.

The people of Iran have conclusively voted in favor of accepting all of the proposals. Under Shah Pahlavi's personal leadership, reform in Iran is developing rapidly and surely.

Persepolis

Persepolis was the pride of Persia 2,500 years ago. The remains that stand today are proudly pointed out as the symbol of influence that Persia's culture occupies in the modern world. Darius the Great, the builder of Persepolis, has often been called the Father of History because of his foresight in establishing a kingdom for future civilizations to study.

To enjoy the Persepolis of old, and the Iran of today, one should plan to be in the ancient city on a holiday. Friday, being a religious holiday, is the best day of the week. The open air and warm sun beckon residents of Shiraz, nearby villages, and tribes to bring their lunches and spend the day. Columns of palaces and stones of 2,500 years ago point their historic heads upward, while happy youths frolic upon the ancient stage. Vibrating rhythms of Iranian music, dominated by drum and flute, are mixed with the pounding rhythm of the western world's twisting sounds. Friendly faces smile an unspoken welcome. And the bolder individuals speak their few words of English, which range from, "I love you," to, "How are you?" Some simply say, "Hello." If the greeting is returned with the same warmth, one is likely to be invited for tea, Pepsi Cola, or Canada Dry orange. Or all three. One may make as many friends as one's bladder will permit.

The brightness of a setting sun or the quiet glow of early morning light enriches the architectural values of Persepolis. From the mountain that rises above the ruins one can survey the ancient city and miles of fertile valley that surround it. Like a sentry scanning the horizon for dust puffs that would indicate possible hostile hordes, one can study the landscape. With a little imagination the piles of rock and ruins come to life. The play of lights and shadows darting into and out of archways and passages, or creating deep images of relief figures carved majestically on the stones, adds animation and primes one's deepest imagination. Voices of real people often blend with one's thoughts to stimulate greater visionary images.

Ruins of Persepolis — late evening.

Persepolis: the Hall of 100 Columns,
with its few remaining erect columns.
In the background is a fertile valley.

13

Modern-day workmen walk through ruins, past carvings of their ancient predecessors.

Beautifully detailed head carving at Persepolis.

Defaced figures. Time eats away at beauty.

Persepolis steps, walls, and columns.

King is protected by umbrellas. Note the eagle.

Column top decoration; animal and caretaker.

Plate 1. Once the glory of Persia,
Persepolis' beauty today lies in
the quality of its uncovered ruins. A
late evening sun enhances the
columns of Apadana Palace.

Plates 2, 3, 4, 5.
Four carvings on the walls
and staircases of
Apadana Palace.

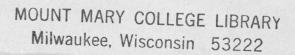

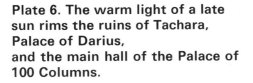

Plate 6. The warm light of a late
sun rims the ruins of Tachara,
Palace of Darius,
and the main hall of the Palace of
100 Columns.

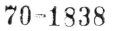

Plate 7. Close-up of a beautifully sculptured head that is carved on one of the walls of Apadana Palace.

Plate 8. Shah Pahlavi hears the proclamation of one of the groups received in audience on Iran's New Year, March 21st. ▶

Plate 9. As the Shah proceeds along the lines of diplomats, ministers, professors, and other important groups and individuals, he comments to some and hears comments from others.

Plate 10. The New Year's audience with the Shah
is one of the important highlights
in the lives of Iranians. Foreigners enjoy the
pomp and color of royalty at work.

Shahanshah Mohammad Reza Pahlavi and Empress Farah.

*Shah, Empress, and the royal children prepare for
a bike ride at the summer palace on the
Caspian Sea.*

King and son, like any father and son, enjoy
playing together.

Salaam and Shahanshah

Lines of automobiles and longer lines of Iranians anxious to catch a glimpse of the Shah, or an important person, make it almost impossible for one to get to the Golestan Palace. The occassion is New Years for Iran, March 21st. And on Now Rooz, as the day is called, Shah Pahlavi holds the annual audience or "Salaam," to greet all of his cabinet ministers, diplomats, and foreign embassy personnel. Golestan Palace's grandeur is given an extra polish for the important event. Royal guards, with helmets gleaming, line the stairwells. Nervous men (there are only a very few women, and these are primarily from the field of education) adjust clothing, smoke, or greet friends infrequently seen since the last Now Rooz. As a group is prepared for the Shah's greeting, the members are ushered into the larger hall, where each person assumes a place in line. When all is ready the doors are opened and the Shah is announced. The Shah hears, and in turn reads, proclamations relating to the group. And following the introduction, he walks slowly down the line, greeting each person in turn. Some of the individuals offer praise or comments, which Shah Pahlavi answers and often punctuates with a smile. Upon completion of a group, the king leaves the room, and a new group is made ready. The pseudo-drama is repeated many times in the five hours of Salaam.

Since Cyrus' kingdom was established in the middle of the sixth century B.C. Persia–Iran has lived under male monarchical rule. Achaemenid, Parthian, Islamic, a series of minor Persian, Ilkhanid and Timurid, Safavid, Zand, Qajar, and Pahlavi dynasties have spanned the twenty-five centuries. Today the second of Pahlavi rulers, Shah Mohammed Reza Pahlavi, rules the country.

Reforms begun by his father, Shah Reza, are continued and new ideas are instituted by the young, progressive king. Opposition and open conflict have punctuated his reign. Attempted assassinations and successful assassinations have highlighted his twenty-five years as monarch. Repulsion of Communist and Russian political and military invasions are apogee points. Land reform and redistribution, improvements in living standards, projects under PLAN Organization, and better foreign relations have also been accomplished by a king who cares for his country and countrymen.

When his marriage to Soraya failed to produce an heir to his throne, Shah Pahlavi married his present wife, the lovely Farah. A Crown Prince and Princess are the fruits of this union.

During a holiday in Babol, on the Caspian Sea, the informal family photographs were taken at the summer palace.

Crown Jewels

Down two flights of stairs beneath Bank Markazi Iran in Tehran and through a huge vault door is one of the world's most dazzling jewel collections. The Crown Jewels of Iran have been collected throughout centuries of history by conquerors, emperors, and kings. Much of the history of Persia and Iran can be coordinated to items in the collection. Great conflicts were often fought over the ownership of a stone, throne, or gem. Many of the jewels and jewel-studded objects have been presented to Shahs and the royal family. And several items have been assembled from loose stones to create rare and priceless objects. The Globe of Gems is a prime example of creating a work of art without price or evaluation.

There are inadequate records regarding the collection until the Safavid period in the late 16th century. During the Third Empire, under Shah Abbas the Great, Persia once again became a united and powerful country. When the Afghans conquered Persia, the jewels were scattered, with some going to India. Shah Nadir brought much of the treasure back following his conquest of India in 1739. Fath-Ali Shah had the Kiani Crown constructed. And the famous Nadir Throne, often referred to as the Peacock Throne, was also built by Fath-Ali Shah. Both are unusual examples of jewelry. The Globe of Gems was added to the collection by Nasser-uddin Shah. Some of the jewels were disposed of by free-spending royalty, but their activities were checked before important pieces were dismantled. In 1938, under the leadership of Shah Reza, the collection was brought to its present location in Bank Melli and transferred to Bank Markazi when it was chartered in 1960.

Tehran

Tehran is a city searching for a personality. To be East or West is the question. It does not know if it wants to remain an Asian city and sparkle as a gem of high brilliance, or adopt entirely the ways of the western world and European thinking, and in so doing be eclipsed by Paris, Rome, and London. There will be many more years before this decision is made, and then the choice might well be wrong. Tehran is an ancient city with a glorious past, but how successful will it be as a modern mecca of the Middle East?

The people continue to cling to traditions of centuries, while ogling the progress of contemporary societies. A flowing chadur, with corner clenched tightly in the mouth holding it firmly over the wearer's head, covers not only the meagerness of the poor but also the unstylishness or bad taste of the middle class. Outlawed in 1936 by Shah Reza, who is considered the founder of modern Iran, the veil, or chadur, remains to remind one of the desire Iranians have to hold onto the past, especially by the uneducated lower-income groups. Religious reasons are most often presented as the purpose for covering the woman's body and most of the face. In this age of enlightenment, women are seldom reluctant about being observed and photographed, while protected by the soft silk-like chadur covering. Chadurs are of many colors, with the larger percentage being made of dark or black material. When the dark colors are worn, the women seem to be nuns when viewed from the hindside. Spring and summer months bring forth gayer colored chadurs.

But underneath the chadur Iranian women are experimenting with western clothing. All too often they fail to understand western apparel. It is not uncommon to see sweaters and skirts mis-matched with cotton stockings and a lightweight pajama-like pants. The pants are twisted and stuffed into the stockings, creating big bulges that distort the shape of legs. High heeled shoes are forced onto feet unaccustomed to tight enclosures. Perhaps the chadur is used as a shield by women uncertain of their appearance. Younger women and teenagers are succeeding in adopting western ways of dress and every day this age group more and more casts aside the chadur.

Men of Tehran have had a somewhat easier transition from ancient ways to modern image. A white shirt is the symbol of status. When a man holds any job that will allow him to wear a white shirt, he considers himself important. He may own only one suit. But he wears that every day with a white shirt. The suit is seldom an expensive one. And it most often is of a vertical stripe. Few Iranian men have mastered the art of wearing casual or sport clothes. And until a better selection of imported clothing is available, Tehran's men will continue to dress nicely, but not well.

Plate 16. The Nadir Throne
stands magnificently at the end
of a row of cases that hold
crowns and the Globe. Called the Peacock Throne (there are three),
it is the product of the
Shah Fath-Ali reign. There are
26,733 gems in the throne, which was
used in the coronation of
Shah Reza in 1925.

Plates 12, 13, 14, 15 (left+below).
Globe of Gems has 51,000 stones,
weighing 18,200 carats,
which are set in a 75 pound gold stand.
The globe is 2 feet in diameter.
Seas are represented with emeralds;
land is indicated by rubies;
diamonds and sapphires form countries, and the equator is lined
with diamonds.

Plates 17, 18 (above).
The case containing a headpiece
worn by the Crown Prince
under Shah Fath-Ali.
Panels of swords and other objects
are in the background.
The hat is surrounded by reflections
of Nadir Throne and Globe of Gems.

Plate 19 . Sea of Light
is the world's largest uncut diamond.
Called Daria-i-Nur,
it is 1½ inches long, an inch wide,
and 3/8ths of an inch thick.
It weighs 182 carats.

Plate 20. A spotlight brilliantly ▶
calls attention to the Pahlavi Crown
and the Sea of Light diamond.
Pahlavi Crown has 3,755 stones
weighing 10,400 carats.

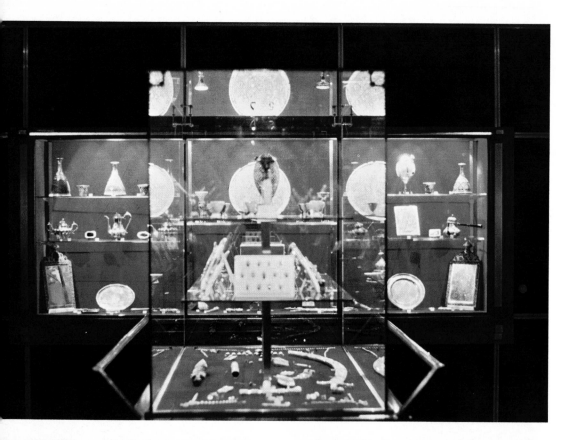

Plate 21. One of many cases containing assorted objects set with stones. Most of the items in this case are covered with turquoise.

Plate 22. Enamel snuff boxes and assorted objects.

Plate 23. The jewels used by members of the royal family include tiaras, necklaces, earrings, bracelets, and brooches.

Plate 24. Candlesticks and other items.

Plate 25. The Kiani Crown was designed and used for the coronation of Fath-Ali Shah Qajar. This is the oldest crown in the collection. ▶

Plate 26. Diamonds ranging in size up to 120 carats and the ''all conquering sword'' of Nadir Shah are the highlights of this case. The case behind houses necklaces and bracelets.

Contrast in modern Tehran.

For centuries Tehran has been a terminal for travelers. Caravans, camel trains, and nomads journeyed to Tehran before going to their final destination. In today's living, Tehran retains this position of importance in addition to being capital of the country. Constant invasion of citizens from all over the country creates, at least at the moment, insurmountable traffic problems.

On any major street one will witness scores of push-carts, donkeys, bicycle riders, pedestrians, and even camels moving or darting among automobiles, motor scooters, and motorcycles. Men and women, with bundles stacked several feet high on their heads, maneuver the crossing of streets seemingly unaware of anyone but themselves. And the entire situation is made even more complex by discourteous and, not too infrequently, illiterate taxi drivers. The aggressiveness of taxi drivers breeds aggressiveness among all drivers as a matter of survival.

If all Iranian drivers were as aggressive toward self-improvement in such areas as personal habits, cleanliness, manners, living conditions, grooming, and good taste as they are in forging their automobiles ahead of other drivers, the country would show an immediate progress. The drivers exert their greatest energies on being "first" when behind the steering wheel. Little energy is left for mending furniture or cleaning the bathroom.

Yet with some of the more obvious faults, Tehran leads the way in reformation and reform. Unfortunately, progress is retarded by lack of understanding and ignorance by older citizens. Shah Pahlavi is following his father's example of educating the masses. Education is the key to Iran's future. As the population is educated, greater improvements can be instituted. An enlightened citizen is an understanding and ambitious citizen. Education among male children continues at a successful pace. But education of female children, even though Shah Reza began the program early in his reign, remains largely unaccepted. Coeducational schooling is almost non-existent.

Education of young girls in Iran is having a difficult time. Recently, in Tehran, two schools were built in one area, one for boys and one for girls. The boy's school was filled to overflowing. But the girl's school had only 80 students the first day. By the end of two weeks there were only 20 left. The remaining 60 had been withdrawn because of religious pressure or unfavorable comments by friends of the parents. The government knows the value of higher education for its people of both sexes and provides physical facilities for instruction. Yet the uneducated older generations are retarding improvements by their reluctance to accept the opinions of more intelligent individuals. It would appear the only way to educate both sexes is to require by law a minimum of 12 years of schooling. The crime would then be in failure to attend school. Now the crime is in the waste of human brain power due to undevelopment.

Public scribe. Street-corner assistance for the illiterate.

Prime Minister Hoveyda in Parliament.

Senate and Parliament in session.

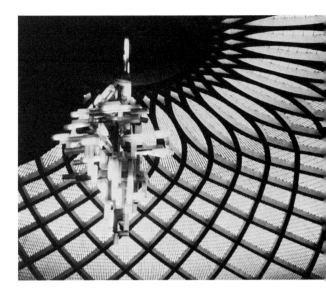

Interior dome and exterior of Senate building.

Medical students at Tehran University.

Today

Knowledgeable Iranians will readily admit that their country has been "asleep for 200 years." Men of government and business recognize that their country has practically stood still while the western world shaped a new civilization. And the fact that critical self-evaluation exists is very healthy.

Not only does the recognition of need for improvement exist, but under the leadership of Shah Pahlavi, his prime ministers, and ministers of various offices, and along with the administration of "Seven Year Development Programs" by PLAN Organization, the country is correcting many of its deficiencies.

PLAN is an independent government organization that serves to supervise the work in four categories of activities: agriculture, communications, industries and mines, and social services. The money for these improvements comes almost entirely from oil revenue.

An Economic Council, with the Shah as chairman, has devised and developed three seven-year programs for increasing the economic stability of Iran. The first program began in 1947. Suffering from lack of experience, the programs were slow at first, but with experience and success, confidence of objectives stimulated the men who guided the programs to greater goals. Among the accomplishments to date are dams for power and reserve water, roads and highways, irrigation and better techniques of farming, increased production of all industrial plants, initiation of new industry, recruiting of foreign industrial investments, better living conditions, and an enforced education program to combat the 76 percent illiteracy. Under PLAN, communications systems have been inaugurated to link all of Iran's remote regions together with telephone, railroads, airports, and television. Hopes are high that television will accelerate the decline of illiteracy through education programs. Lethargy and indifference are gradually disappearing, even though there are times when no positive action is taking place. And there are areas where minor improvements are considered major accomplishments. The most overrated improvements are in roads.

For a country that is the fourth largest oil producer in the world, Iran's roads are inadequate and often impassable. One would think that availability of oil and asphalt products would insure the construction of good roads. But, with few exceptions, such is not the case. Major highway arteries between principal cities are seldom more than two-laned semi-completed asphalt roads. And between smaller towns and villages rough, dusty, rock or dirt trails serve as roads. Neither the good roads or the not so good trails are properly cared for. Dangerous mountain curves have no protective guard rails, heavy snows or rain-softened mountainsides lie in wait for the unsuspecting before becoming an avalanche with no measures to restrict them, and streams are allowed to flow across roadbeds, eating away the foundation and causing more roughness.

There is, unfortunately, a scarcity of gas and service stations. The convenience of gas stations with toilet facilities is only found in larger villages and towns. There are scores of miles through flat, uninhabited desert land where only sheep and their shepherd, with an occasional vehicle, travel. Should one have automobile difficulty while journeying across a section of desert, he would be at the fate of passersby, if they should come.

Driving in Iran is lonely. Highways are adequate, but certainly need improvement. Secondary roads are unreasonably bad, and third-class roads are a hazard to the vehicles that travel them. And there are endless miles of emptiness. So alone does one feel when the monotonous miles are traveled, the passing of another vehicle will cause a conversation of many minutes. The presence of another human prompts detailed discussion of the automobile and its riders. And there are no official highway police patrols to attend needs of motorists or to regulate and enforce laws of the road.

Although giant steps have been taken in connecting villages, towns, and cities by construction of basic roads, progress is slow and proposed highway projects will take time. Work is under way on several highways, but no completion dates have been established. The government is cognizant of the need for better surface travel, which will stimulate better and faster trade between communities. Under PLAN the roads will be constructed.

Then the problem will be to educate the drivers for safer, more courteous travel.

Nomadic shepherd watches his sheep.

Nomad man with the hat of his tribe.

Nomads — the timeless life: sheep- and goat-herding, carpet weaving, and (opposite) just sitting.

School for nomad children. The teacher and tent travel with the tribes.

Nomad woman and child await medical inspection.

Malaria control. The government inspector examines a nomadic family, whose goat-hair tent has been code-marked for identification.

Blood test for a child too young to take enough medicated salt.

Nomads

There is an honesty existing within Iran's nomadic tribes that is simple and direct. They like or hate. If they like a person, there is an open demonstration of approval. Conversely, if they hate a person, the display is equally, or perhaps more, aggressive.

The nomads live according to their own code. The "Huns" are the leaders and are often referred to as parasites because they glean their income from the labors of tribesmen. But Huns are owners of land, and their ownerships are handed down through generations. They also serve a major function as providers and arbitrators between families when arguments arise. Because of the respect and devotion the Huns enjoy, their decisions and rulings are seldom questioned.

In lands where nomads have winter and summer quarters, there are vast acres uninhabited except for tent-quartered tribes. In an effort to get these tribes to settle and till the land, the government constructed "villages" of adobe homes where the sheep were usually grazed. The nomads wanted no part of the confinement imposed by communal living. And the villages, which were never occupied, stand now in ruins as testimony to an abortive governmental attempt to alter a way of life established over centuries. Local residents point to the decayed buildings and call them "monuments." The tribes prefer their tents of goat's hair.

In winter, tribes occupy rich valleys in southwest Iran. The green flat lands are surrounded by rocky, treeless, and often snow-clad mountains. Rock slides are not uncommon in the spring. So vast are the valleys that a man can be absorbed into the land without a trace. Men can stand so quietly that their shapes become part of the rocks, stones, and puffs of black bush terrain, unnoticed by inexperienced outsiders. From their unobtrusive observation post they watch the sheep scamper over rocks and boulders in search of grass. As the sheep move they make a rustling sound like water hurrying over a shallow creekbed. At the rear of the flock run the always faithful dogs, keeping the sheep together, and protected.

The tribesman is alternately a good and bad man. An encounter we had on a road during daylight hours is an example. Our jeep had a flat tire and we needed assistance in repairing it. A passing truck, loaded with nomad males, stopped. The men fixed the tire, smiled, and waved a warm farewell. But, our guide said, "At night the same men would have robbed or killed us." Prevailing law in the unpoliced, sparsely populated regions is one of survival of the strongest. After dark, the policy is to shoot first and ask questions later. And because of the bigness of unsettled lands, anyone outside the law can forever be hidden if the tribes choose to hide him.

Improvements in living conditions for the tribes are being made. Under the direction of UNICEF and Iran's Malaria Eradication Program, the inhabitants are being given medicated salt, blood tests, and instructions in better health through control of sanitation. Malaria is almost under control.

The health program is not only helping to eliminate malaria but simultaneously is educating the people. Of course, one is optimistic to think that immediate alterations can be made in the personal hygiene habits of uneducated people. Constant contact and vigilance have rewarded malaria workers with partial success and given hope for greater successes. But convincing a tribesman that a slit trench for body waste is more desirable than depositing excrement on the ground, where flies and other insects will breed, is difficult if not impossible. The tribesmen do not have enough education to understand the medical reasons.

To prepare tribal youths for a better future and to give them a basic six grades of elementary education, the government is providing teachers with tents so they may travel with the tribes. Where failure marked the attempt to settle tribes, success prevails in inaugurating an educational program. Children who would otherwise remain illiterate are now having the benefit of at least six years of education. This basic knowledge will aid them to understand suggestions made by workers such as those in the malaria control and hygiene programs.

Even the education program suffers from the shortage of qualified personnel. Seldom is the teacher educated beyond six grades himself. Usually a teacher is a member of the tribes and is often disadvantaged in instituting new or different ideas and methods because of his own limited knowledge or his involvement as a tribesman. He is handicapped in teaching or advocating changes that he does not endorse or understand himself. But this small beginning offers hope. And with perseverance by dedicated workers who have devoted their lives to the tribes' health and welfare, living standards will rise to new and greater heights.

Nomads were offered land but did not take advantage of Shah Pahlavi's Land Redistribution Program. Under the law, receipt of government distributed lands requires settling permanently on the land and farming it. Nomads refuse to take permanent residence anywhere, as evidenced by the village ruins, preferring to change tent sites as the weather changes. So the tribes continue to live under the same rules, codes, and conditions that have controlled tribal life for generations—centuries.

Yet one cannot help but admire these people. Their simple, uncluttered way of life breeds a mentally healthy atmosphere. There is none of the indecision of conduct that is frustrating the populations of Iran's cities. The ways of the past are still strong. And changes will be hard-fought.

Fishermen at market on Caspian Sea.

On a calm day, the saturated blue of the Caspian Sea, the world's largest inland lake, swells rhythmically and rolls its moderate waves onto sandy shores. Conversely, on a stormy day the sea slams the breakers violently against the shoreline. The sky turns from blue to green and to grey-black. And on violent days, Caspian fishermen remain in their ports, mending nets, or preparing gear for the calmer days.

Fishing is Iran's third largest industry. From the waters of the Caspian Sea come three major varieties of fish: sturgeon, herring, and whitefish. Of the three, sturgeon, which produces caviar, is the biggest commercial fish. Caviar is exported to America, Russia, and Europe in that order. Twenty-one tons of caviar were shipped to America in one year. Lesser amounts go to Russia and other European countries. From Bandar-Shah to Pahlavi, the southern waters of the Caspian Sea offer a plentiful volume of caviar-producing sturgeon.

In the town of Pahlavi is located the processing plant for all fish. In cold storage rooms that are about 30° below zero, fish are frozen, machine-sliced, and prepared for overseas shipment. Herring is smoked, salted, and packaged. Caviar is canned for foreign countries, and whitefish is processed for home consumption. In addition to preparing fish for market, the Iranian Fisheries Company engages in research for improving the industry. Habits and health of Caspian fish are logged and studied.

Because of proximity to Russia along Caspian shores, where that nation's people lived and ruled for centuries, the costumes of northern Iran retain striking resemblances to Russian dress. Women wear pants and wrap-around shawls that have a marked Russian peasant look.

Water is more plentiful and vegetation is greener. Rice paddies run to shorelines, and contour planting climbs hillsides. Every available acre of land is cultivated. Straw huts serve as rice storage and homes, too. And there seems to be a more industrious attitude among the people.

Two provinces that border Caspian Sea shores are populated with resorts and hotels for vacationing and pleasure-seeking Iranians. Ramsar and Babolsar have both luxury hotels and gambling casinos. Both towns, as well as villages all along the seashore, entertain large influxes of people from April to November.

Fish in preparation for processing at cannery.

Iran's chief caviar-maker.

Sturgeon in cold storage being readied for shipment.

Caspian fishermen and merchants display prize catch.

Rice paddies stretch along the seashore; their furrows are turned by ancient wooden plows behind oxen, and by modern self-propelled machines.

Terraced fields climb the hillsides.

Straw-roofed huts serve as homes and rice-storage barns.

An expressive fisherman directing net loading.

Caspian fisherman and his boat.

Russian influence — in apparel — shows in this woman's shawl.

The shores of the Caspian are lined with resorts and hotels to accommodate vacationing Iranians. Shown here is the Ramsar Hotel.

70

Oil, Abadan, Khorramshahr

Oil is Iran's chief economic force. Since British investments in exploration, drilling, refining, and marketing of Persian oil began in 1901, petroleum has played an important role in Iran's destiny. Until 1926 Persia received no royalties and only then began getting 16 percent. The refinery, which British interests constructed, remains the largest in the world. At one time 300,000 barrels of oil were refined each day. After nationalization of the oil company in 1951, there were three years when the refinery did not process a single barrel of oil. Mechanical and technical reasons are given for this expensive lapse of production time.

Five years after taking over the oil business, Iranian engineers finally drilled their first oil well. All previous wells had been discovered by Englishmen on leased properties. But in 1956, near the city of Ghom, a gusher well was brought in, and Iran could claim its own oil on its own property. Exploration and drilling continues in this area, which is only 125 miles from Tehran. Drilling rigs are visible on the horizon as one drives through the Central province.

Abadan is a city built around a refinery. Primarily populated by employees of the National Iranian Oil Company, the city resembles all other company settlements in the world. Work and play are conducted with the spires of cat-crackers and refining towers as background. Abadan is reached either by canoe–ferry or over the newly completed toll bridge. Most natives take the canoe.

Khorramshahr is the twin city to Abadan. Only the river Kuran separates them. Ocean-going ships dock at Khorramshahr's wharves. Rail and road facilities, which are lacking in other coastal cities, make Khorramshahr the only major world port in Iran.

The tropical climate of the Persian Gulf environs make both Abadan and Khorramshahr very hot in the summer. Temperatures well over 100 degrees Fahrenheit are not uncommon from May to September. Palm trees form groves of green. Flat skylines are interrupted by ship's masts and palm branches.

And all the while the pulse of Persian economy is processing oil, the blood of the country's financial health.

World's largest refinery. Abadan.

*Tin hats, turbans, and bare heads
—refinery workers.*

Oil flows; the turban-wearers sleep.

Before the refinery, a worker paints a white line — by hand.

A quicker pace.

A canoe-ferry slips past ships of the Iranian fleet.

The long canoe glides through the harbor . . .

to join others at Khorramshahr.

Palm Grove park. Abadan.

Swift horse. Slow water.

Fine Art

Art plays a major part in the lives of Iranians. Ownership of fine carpets and metal crafts is considered a measure of one's wealth. To the non-Iranian, old Persian art and modern Iranian art are objects of beauty, and ownership is undertaken with great pride. Miniature paintings, ceramics, silver and copper ware, carpets, and tiles are beautiful and distinctively Iranian.

From pre-historic times Persian art has influenced world art. Discoveries from 1000 B.C. indicate the quality of craftsmanship. When Islamic rule forbade the portrayal of human figures, sculpture declined, but ceramics, metal crafts, and the painting of animals and geometric designs increased.

In 1900, Kamal-ul-Mulk, who was an artist of distinction, began his own school. His work, and the work of his students, had acceptable recognition. With his reputation established, it was not unusual that Kamal-ul-Mulk's new school should be chosen as the basis of a newly formed Department of Fine Arts.

Two major Fine Arts schools exist. One is in Tehran, where the imposing structure of PLAN Organizations headquarters dwarf the conventional-looking single-story building. The other is in Isfahan, where a relatively new contemporary building, which was designed and constructed by Germans, houses the education of young talented male students.

Work in miniature painting, drawing, sculpture, woodcraft, khatam (inlay of metal and camel bone), ceramics, pottery, and carpet weaving prepare the students for a professional life in art.

The products of arts and crafts are offered in bazaars throughout Iran, and many items are exported throughout the world. The sale of Iranian artifacts forms the second largest source of income in the country. From small shopkeepers who make their saleable merchandise on the premises to full-time workers in Tehran's Fine Arts Department art enjoys a high position in the national economy. And artists are respected as outstanding citizens.

Artist in Department of Fine Arts working on plate painting.

Fine Arts building is dwarfed by PLAN headquarters structure.

Interior of Fine Arts building.

Inside, workers file camel bone for inlays.

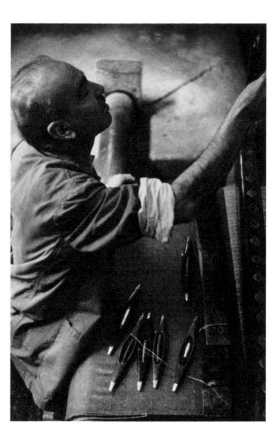

*Weaving Persian carpets — Department of
Fine Arts.*

People

 Iranians are at once friendly, warm, generous; and reserved, hostile, and resentful. Such a mixture of emotion has been bred in two generations of economic, social, and cultural frustration. Contemporary Persians, like their historical counterparts, are a proud people. After centuries of leading world civilization, it is not an easy thing to accept an inferior position. And not all Iranians are accepting the role. There are 20,000 students in universities and colleges abroad; most will return to assume their place in today's society. Unfortunately, many will not, because greater financial rewards are to be gained in foreign lands. And many will not return because of social customs long in need of alteration, especially in the relationships between the sexes.

Social life among young adults and teenagers in Iran is in an unfortunate and undesirable state. An age-old philosophy of complete separation of sexes until marriage continues to control the relationships of the sexes. Marriages are negotiated. And it is not uncommon to find a fifteen-year-old girl married to a fifty-year-old man. Older generations may consent to this arrangement, but young men are seldom in agreement with the seemingly unalterable situation. Certainly, among young men who have traveled to Europe or America for their education, there is a great desire to have friendly social associations with members of the opposite sex without the altar as the objective. Because these men have been exposed to the pleasure of making casual friendships with young women on a purely social basis, having to accept the restrictions of Iranian traditions is difficult. Social dating is taboo. Occasionally, some friendship dating will be observed in Tehran. But such activity is unheard of in any other city. Perhaps the worst consequence of the restricted boy/girl relationship is the forcing of men to assume a role normally relegated to females.

In one city we had occasion to spend several evenings with young men of university age and academic background. During the evening they danced together. One man played the woman's role as dancing partner. It is not a happy situation to watch men in their late twenties and early thirties behaving in a psuedo-girlish manner. Because young women are denied the privilege of being entertained by men, for fear of social stigma, the males are forced to behave in unmasculine ways.

Couple the desire of Iranian youth for broader social activities with a knowledge of what is happening in Europe and America as seen in movies and television, and you have the frustration present in today's young people. There exists in all humans the desire to express affection for the opposite sex. If this expression cannot be channeled in the right direction, it might well be misdirected. One of the alternates would be in a stronger homosexual relationship. It is not uncommon to see men strolling the street holding hands, or fondling and caressing each other while engaged in conversation. The behavior is identical to that which is most often demonstrated between different sexes.

Perhaps contemporary Iranian men feel completely justified in displaying affection to other males because of hand-holding monarchs and leaders of empires of centuries past. On Persepolis' walls there are many carvings that show warriors, kings, and outstanding citizens holding hands in peaceful union. The symbol of joining forces in peacefulness is the indication. There was no affection as is most often the case in today's hand-holding Iranian men.

The social problem is complex, and there is no easy solution. Allowing young girls to mix socially with men of their own ages is made an acute situation because of two factors. One is lack of emotional preparation of the girl. And, two, is the inability of older generations to comprehend the meaning of social friendship.

There has not been a gradual maturing of physical and emotional attitude in young girls to allow them to cope with the sudden freedom they may acquire. Consequently, among young girls who have been permitted a more liberal association with young men, there is a high percentage of misconduct. Lack of proper orientation on behavior has all too often led to a girl's getting more involved than she intended. But where does behavior instruction begin? The home is hardly the right place, for all too few parents know what is expected in conduct because they never had experience in such situations. A mother cannot instill in a daughter correct social conduct to which she herself is a stranger. Creating confidence in the daughter requires the mother to be confident. The mother has never associated with unmarried men on a "good friends" basis, and is therefore limited in her ability to instruct.

To fill the gap between complete orientation and limitation of the parents, planned programs of instruction will have to be instituted. The government can include social instruction in the required first six years of elementary education, and more coeducational schools must be started. Within the school program, instruction in hygiene, moral conduct, grooming, self respect, and examples of manners in other countries, which could be used as guides for changes, could be integrated into the present curriculum. Schools would be made responsible for conducting classes on how to associate with contemporaries of the opposite sex. And to create the right atmosphere, gatherings such as parties and dances would be held under school auspices. With educational authorities displaying acceptance of boy/girl togetherness without the stigma of misconduct, parents would alter their attitudes.

In Tehran there is a small degree of adjustment being made in boy/girl relationships. But breaking tradition is hard. And many of the young women who are allowed to enjoy the company of young men are labled "bad" girls. Unfortunately, many very proper young ladies must bear the inaccurate evaluation. When customs are changed pioneers often suffer the abuse of their peers who cannot, or do not want to, understand the true motives. But, in spite of undesirable labels that have been registered against the non-conformist youngsters, these few are helping to clear the way for future freedoms. When Tehran has a broader acceptance of contemporary social relationships between the sexes, the attitude will spread to the towns and villages, and ultimately throughout the country. But, as one Tehranian stated, "It could take 5, 50, or 500 years."

The 22.5 million people of Iran span the spectrum of work, activities, and professions. In business or in the home, Iranians conduct themselves in patterns established over centuries. A sign of friendship is the offering of tea. And when the best Persian carpets are spread for a visitor, the act may be considered one of genuine welcome.

Persians are patient. One intelligent man offered this explanation. "When you have been around three or four thousand years what is a year or two?" Another man said it this way. "If the practice is good enough for 75 or 100 years, it is good enough to continue."

Chadur covers all but one eye.

Eastern mother and western child. Tehran.

Water pipe, called "babble-bubble" by Iranians.

Father and son, shopkeepers.

Nomadic tribeswomen, entering Persepolis for festival.

Sewing baby shoes. A finished shoe is pinned to the woman's headdress, for future reference.

Faces — Persian workmen.

Traffic. Policeman fights weary battle with camels, sheep, pedestrians, pushcarts, bicycles, and vehicles.

Chadur-clad women and double-decker bus. Tehran.

Chadur-covered bridal party at Persepolis.

Employment. Government official; small shop owner; door-to-door salesman. Tehran.

Iranian women. Change comes slowly.

Shah Pahlavi, Empress Farah, and other members of the royal family at a formal dinner and reception.

Prime Minister, cabinet ministers, and members of the diplomatic corps attend the Shah's audience.

Modern Tehran housing.

Downtown Tehran at dusk.

Interior of a well-decorated taxi.

Tehran street encounter. Woman stops to give alms, then continues on her way as beggar calculates her generosity.

As Tehran expands, it takes on a more
European-American look.

Older architecture is seen in the
Parliament building, but new structures
— office buildings, banks, apartment
houses — take contemporary forms.

113

Shiraz

Quran Gate, entrance to Shiraz.

Shiraz, Iran's third most important city, is located in the southern
section of the country. The plain on which the city is set is surrounded
by high mountains. At an elevation of 5,000 feet the climate is at once
pleasant, tropical, and stimulating. Entrance into Shiraz is through
the Allah-o-Akbar pass, down a long grade, and through the Quran
Gate. As one approaches the gate, all of the city is spread before him.

Quran Gate was first constructed over 1,000 years ago as both a
means of protecting the entrance to the city and as an ornamental
edifice to dispel the evil-eye from the city. A relatively new gate stands
today where the old one was destroyed 25 years ago. Above the arch-
way, inscribed in Farsi, is "Welcome." Until recently a huge Koran
rested on the topmost point of the gate. Belief was that all who passed
through the gate passed beneath the protection of the holy word. The
100-pound Bible is now in Pars Museum, but the belief in divine protection continues.

While beauty of setting and excellence of climate qualify Shiraz
for attention, the city's major claim to fame is two of its former residents. Persia's world-famous poets Sa'di and Hafiz called Shiraz their
home. Hafiz never left the city, while Sa'di wandered the known
world of his time only to find the peace and contentment he sought
in his native city. Prose and poetry of Sa'di are recognized the world
over as philosophical, lyrical, and witty, and his understanding of
people and life in the 13th century A.D. is very applicable in today's
world. The verse opening this chapter could well apply to civil rights
or struggles of young African nations.

Even though Shiraz has never regained the eminence it experienced
from 879 to 902 A.D. when the Safavids made the city capital of the
country, it has not stood still economically, politically, or culturally.

Art, handicrafts, textiles, and modern factories combine to increase the economic activity of Shiraz's 250,000 inhabitants. And
annually new industrial plants commence operation to exploit the
natural resources of Shiraz and the surrounding territory.

Yet amid the ambitions to achieve greater industrialization, men
who shape the city's destiny retain a regard for beauty. Long have the
gardens of Shiraz been sung about in the poems of Sa'di and Hafiz
and other writers. And the beauty of the gardens is never overrated.
Semi-tropical climate is conducive to beautiful vegetation. When modern construction is undertaken, provisions for landscaping and gardens are primary in the planning.

Tomb of Shiraz poet Sa'di.

Tomb of the poet Hafiz. Young men enter the shrine, holding hands.

A mosque is repaired. The workmen and a little boy rest.

Masjid Nau, the largest mosque in Persia. Shiraz.

Mir Mohammad Mosque in Shiraz.

Isfahan

Isfahan is a city that can be seen in three days. But what is viewed will take years to appreciate fully. Beauty is defined by the observation of Isfahan. From bridges that span the river to mosques pointed skyward to shabbily clad children, Isfahan is a testimony to its heritage. The glory of Persia's Third Empire, when Isfahan was the capital, remains evident in buildings and art. Everywhere art and artists may be observed. Tappings of small hammers held by busy hands rhythmically beat out designs on silver, copper, and brass. Quietly, the brush of a painter of miniatures lays its images onto camel bone or shell. A southern sun highlights mosaic tiles that decorate the horizon as they form roofs and walls for mosques. Isfahan has managed to retain its sophisticated character even though it has lost political ground.

The natives of Isfahan say that their city is half the world. When one has witnessed Isfahan's beauty, there is little else anywhere worth seeing. From on top Shah Mosque the panorama of mud-roofed brown buildings in their earth color reaches to the mountains. Globe-shaped mosques are visible in all directions, breaking the rectangular forms of homes and schools.

The noise of a city continuing its commercial ways includes taxi horns, camel train bells, vendor's chants, and bare wheels of push carts against rock streets. But the noises are never distractions from the city's art. Sights and sounds blend.

The traveler, much like Hajji Baba, who was the hero of James Morier's book, is impatient to return to Isfahan. Once visited, the magic of the city beckons for an immediate return. Unlike Hajji Baba, the traveler does not need to be a native to marvel at the art, architecture, and handicraft.

Isfahan's recorded history dates back over 2000 years. The Muslims captured the city in 644 A.D. Since that date the city has kept its Islamic name while retaining Persian appearance and architecture. Under the Safavid Dynasty, and Shah Abbas, Isfahan received lasting fame as the Iranian capital. Until 1722, when the last Safavid king was overthrown by the Afghans, Isfahan flourished as the country's center of arts, industry, and trade.

The city's half million population acts out its daily duties on the stages of mosaic mosques and historic squares (maidans). Maidan Shah is the center of all activity. Bazaars, merchants, camel trains, children, students, and chadur-clad women, who are but a part of the inhabitants, spend at least some of their day in the beauty of Maidan Shah, which was once the Shah's polo field.

Waterpipe smokers on Isfahan street.

Isfahan:
Chehel Sotoon Palace
at night.

Interior of Shaykh Lotfollah Mosque.

Looking out from teashop on
Maidan Shah.

124

Maidan Shah — activity.

Isfahan — street scene.

Downstream from a 1000-year-old bridge, women wash clothes, dishes, and vegetables.

The Armenian Museum; exterior and interior.

Persian manuscript, in Armenian Museum, over 1000 years old.

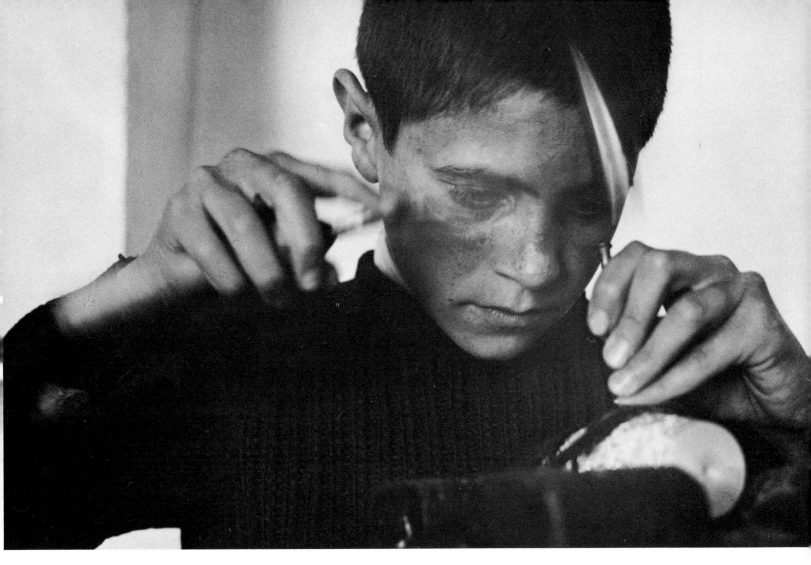

Young fine arts student hammers silver cup.

Inlay frame-makers in Shiraz.

Sculpture class, Isfahan School of Fine Arts.

Decorative tile-work on Fars Palace in Shiraz.

Haj Mosauer-al-Molki, last of Persia's great miniaturists.

Enamelist at Isfahan Fine Arts School.

Landscapes

I ran is three times the size of France, covers as much territory as a half dozen mid-western American states, and is two-thirds desert. A few minutes drive south from Tehran and one is entering desert land. Major cities exist because of their proximity to water. Green skylines of city oases never fail to thrill an approaching traveler.

On the vast lands that exist from low to very high elevation, one can see camel trains moving slowly toward their destination, sheep grazing, oil well rigs, and clay-constructed communities accentuated by a mosque's dome. Deserts are at once empty, barren, desolate, challenging, beautiful, and sensuous.

Secrets of centuries lie within the towering peaks of mountains that have looked down on vanished civilizations. And wind-blown sands have erased traces of cities or villages that lie beneath the desert. The hot quietness of a denuded desert or the silence of snow-capped mountains stimulate the viewer to imagine how they might have been a thousand or 5000 years ago.

A camel train on the desert south of Tehran.

*Near Ghom, an asphalt road leads to an
oil well; an irrigation ditch leads to a mosque.*

*Massive, expansive, and
uninhabited — two thirds of the
Iranian landscape. Deserted
government housing for Nomads,
above, and a clay construction
community, right, abut sensuous,
bare, eroded hills.*

140

Night Life

For twenty dollars a party of four can enjoy dinner and an uninterrupted four-hour floor show at one of Tehran's first-class night clubs. Chelow Kabab, Chicken Kabab, wine, and fruit are served in generous portions. Of equal portions are the singers, musicians, and belly dancers. A large percentage of Tehran's entertainment is imported from Europe. But there is an ample mixture of local talent. Belly dancing is native to the Middle East and is very popular with the night set. Three clubs lead the list of Tehran's night life: Shokufeh-Now, Miami, and Moulin Rouge. Perhaps the popularity of night life results from the limited home entertainment. There are only a few hours of television, and most homes are too small for much entertainment. These may be the reasons why many adults spend as many as five nights a week in night clubs.

Plate 27. A student is reflected in the
Maidan Shah fountain with the reflected background of Lutfullah Mosque.

Plate 28. Sḥah Mosque tilework
on dome is among the finest.
Built at the beginning
of the seventeenth century under the
reign of Shah Abbas.

Plate 29 (right).
The oldest mosque is Jum'a,
which is 1,000 years old.

Plate 30 (below).
Inside courtyard of Jum'a
mosque a youngster takes
a drink.

Plate 35. A carpet maker of Isfahan.
The city remains the center
of the carpet industry even though
industrialization of textile factories
has taken place.

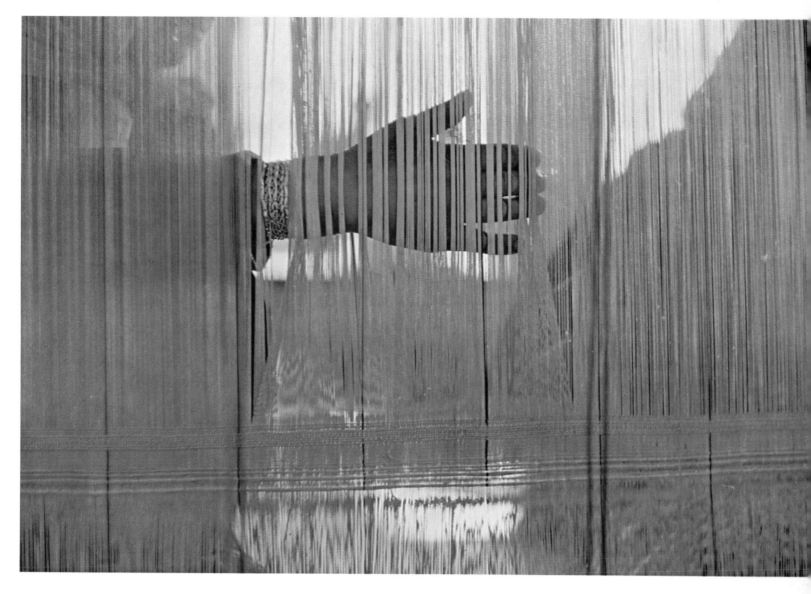

Plate 31. A Fountain adds to the beauty of
the cream-colored
Sheikh Lutfullah Mosque.

Plate 32. Basking in a warm southern sun
the dome of Sheikh Lutfullah's
cream-colored mosque is one of Isfahan's
most memorable landmarks.

Plate 33. The Chahasbagh mosque,
which is a theological school, is the last
building constructed by the
Safavid rulers.

Plate 34. Prayer time in
Shah Mosque of Tehran, one of the most
beautiful in Iran.

Plate 36. A shopkeeper/artist hammers
a large copper tray with the aid of his
son. This is a typical scene in Maidan Shah.

**Plate 37. In the school of Fine Arts
a professor hammers delicate designs on a
silver bowl.**

Plate 38. Most of the arts and crafts
are sold in the bazaars of Tehran, Shiraz and
Isfahan. Objects of gold and silver,
copper or brass are on display and are
available at a good price. Bargaining for the
price is part of the fun.

Bazaar

The bazaar is a way of life, and those engaged in it appear to enjoy living. Except for the merchandise, little has changed in the bazaars of Iran's principal cities of Tehran, Isfahan, and Shiraz. Day and night the constant clamor of buyers and merchants fills the air.

The bazaar of Tehran is the largest in Iran and perhaps the largest in the Middle East. Narrow cave-like tunnels wind endlessly. One may enter the honeycomb of shops and walk for hours only to emerge a few feet down the street from where the entrance was made. Telephone-booth-size shops offer every item one can name. Most of the shops specialize in one line of merchandise. And there is usually a concentration of shops selling similar items. Carpets, shoes, art and handicrafts, jewelry, cloths, and clothing are to be found assembled near each other.

In daylight hours there is an underground atmosphere because of limited light filtering through canopied structures. At night a carnival-like midway effect is created as neon signs and portable oil burning lanterns are set ablaze. Hawkers bellowing bids for buyers and the hum of hundreds of people in search of products, necessities, or luxuries combine for a chorus of bargain basement music. Women, with their chadurs clenched between their teeth, gesture disapprovingly at a merchant who wants more money than the buyer is willing to pay. Hands wave. Faces express thoughts. And in the end a sale is made with both parties satisfied. Bargaining over the price of goods is part of the performance. If the asking price is paid, the merchant thinks the buyer a fool. If there is no exchange of opinions about price, some of the fun of bazaar buying is left out of the transaction.

The Isfahan bazaar centers around the Maidan Shah. Under a dome-like tunnel the major section of the bazaar resembles old castle corridors. Round holes overhead permit shafts of light to cut through the inky darkness. But the bargaining over merchandise is conducted in the same manner as in Tehran. On the square itself are many craftsmen–merchants, who create the goods they sell while waiting on, or waiting for, customers. Small streets that serve as arteries to the square are lined with shops offering many of the hand-wrought metal objects for which Isfahan is famous.

On a much smaller scale than either Tehran or Isfahan, the bazaar of Shiraz is set in a single high-ceilinged building. Metal sliding doors cover the fronts of individual shops. When business is closed, the doors are pulled down and locked, which makes a cell-block looking row of openings.

Tehran's bazaar is concentrated near Meydan Ark and the Golestan Palace. Portable stalls line the streets leading to the major section of the bazaar. One cannot walk on a street without finding fruits, vegetables, nuts, lottery tickets, cigarettes, flowers, and mirrors offered for sale.

When planning a trip through any of the bazaars in Iran, one must allow plenty of time. There is an endless variety of merchandise to inspect, even if one is not buying. The merchants enjoy a discussion

Turkeys in the street. Tehran bazaar.

of their wares. And since many items are made on the spot, the shopper has the opportunity to watch his future possession being made. The lack of a common language does not lessen the excitement of shopping in the bazaar catacombs. It is surprising what hand signals and facial expressions will communicate.

Bizarre bazaar life of Iran is lively and stimulating. Even in contemporary life one can envision how the gigantic 5 & 10 cent variety store-like setting must have appeared in centuries past.

Bazaar at Shiraz.

In the Tehran bazaar — business and sociability, day and night.

157

Carpets.

Mirrors.

Sweets.

Billowing chadur covers western clothing of a shopper in the bazaar.

Plate 39. A popular belly-dancer at the Moulin Rouge Club. ▶

Plate 40. The jingle of camel-train bells echoes along
the walls of the famous Khajoo Bridge as the sun outlines animals
and people crossing. Archways indicate rooms
where nobles and courtiers once contended for attention.

Plate 41. Early morning light begins to illuminate Khajoo Bridge as night lights still glow. Under Safavid rule the bridges played a major role in social life. Khajoo Bridge was also used as a dam on which boating regattas were held. Attendance at a regatta was accompanied by pomp and gaiety. Dancers, singers, and musicians contributed to the lavish life.

Plate 42. Marnon Bridge at sunrise.

Plate 43. Zurkhaneh is a performance
of traditional exercises that
have been enacted through the ages.
Calisthenics with huge dumb-bells, wooden
slabs, chains, and boards are
performed to the rhythmical beat of
a drummer.

Plates 44, 45, 46. In the town of Rey, carpet washing is a daily ritual. New carpets are washed repeatedly to insure permanency of dyes. Family carpets are washed. And all of them are spread on the barren rock cliffs to dry. Hundreds of people take part in the daily drama.

Plate 47. The Chadur is still worn by a large percentage of Iranian women even though Shah Reza has decreed it unlawful. In this picture eyes smile while the rest of the face is hidden.

Plates 48, 49, 50. Golestan Palace in Tehran looks like
a palace. The interiors glitter and shimmer from all
of the gold and glass. Huge chandeliers hang from the ceiling.
One of the Peacock Thrones sits statuesquely at the end
of the great hall. Gem-studded carvings of peacocks
decorate the headboard while cobra-shaped legs support the
bed-like throne.

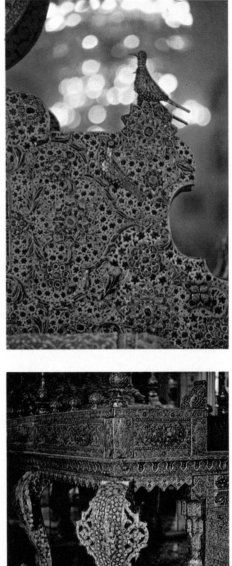

Chadur clenched tight, a woman shops in a bazaar.

Wooden-sword-armed warrior.

Boy Scouts at first aid tent for holidayers in Persepolis.

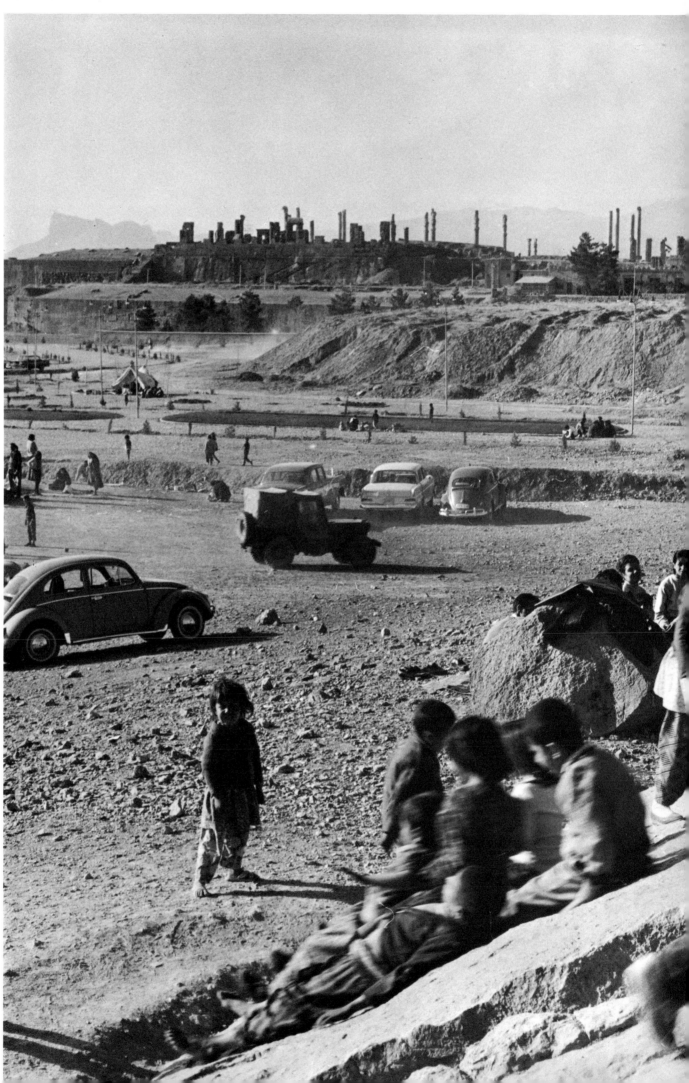

Children. Persepolis.

In Shiraz, in Chalus, in Borazjan, boys grow up.

174

Verbal combat in Shiraz.

Young girls in city park, Tehran.

For a few coins . . . . Kazaroon.

School yard. Isfahan.

Children

Whether sliding down a flat rock at Persepolis, herding sheep on southern plains, or walking along the road in the rain, children of Iran are not unlike children all over the world. They play at imaginary games, fight unreal foes, quarrel with each other, travel to distant lands in daydreams, and earn coins doing pseudo-important jobs.

Perhaps the major difference in Iranian children lies in their future. Because their government is concerned about their welfare, schools and education are on the increase, health programs have been initiated, and more and better employment will be available to them with greater increase in industrialization.

Prayer.

Local musicians, formally called Haji Firouz, entertain children.

Adults invite them into their homes and have an impromptu party.

Persian Fire Temple, built by
Zoroastrians near Isfahan. PLAN is now
constructing a reservoir on the same site.

Excavation work at Persepolis and
other locations continues to reveal
important finds.

A job with prestige: the royal guard.

Lottery ticket salesman.

Sidewalk sewing shop. Making awnings.

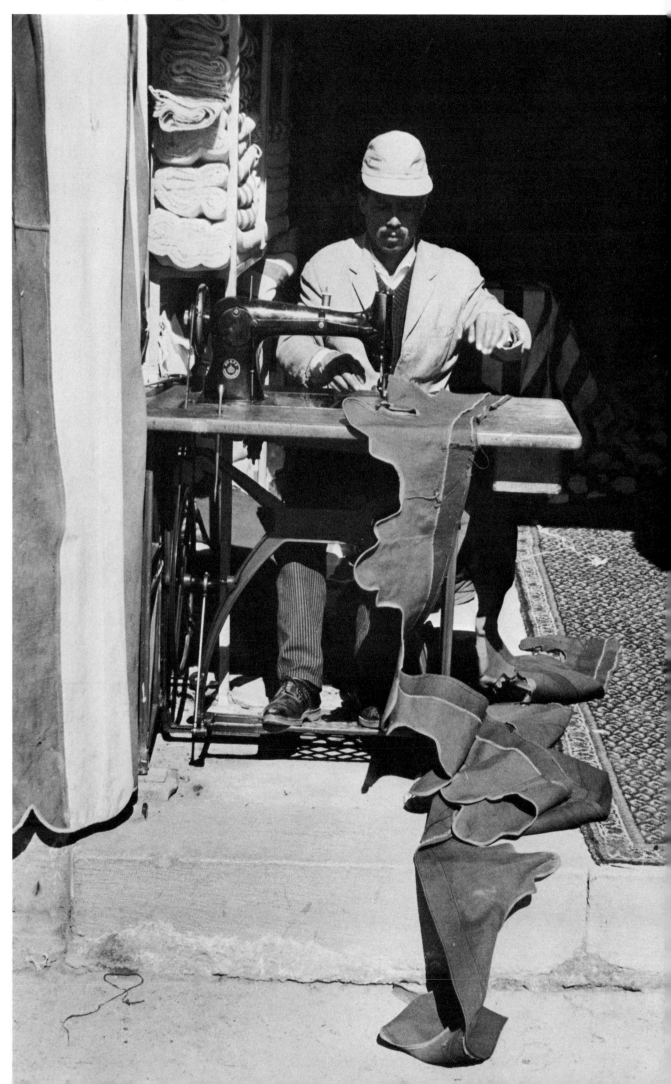

Sefid Rud dam and tunnel for highway,
built under PLAN, indicate the extent of
Iran's accomplishments.

Toward the future — the new road through Manzandaran province.